THE IRISH BIRTHDAY BOOK

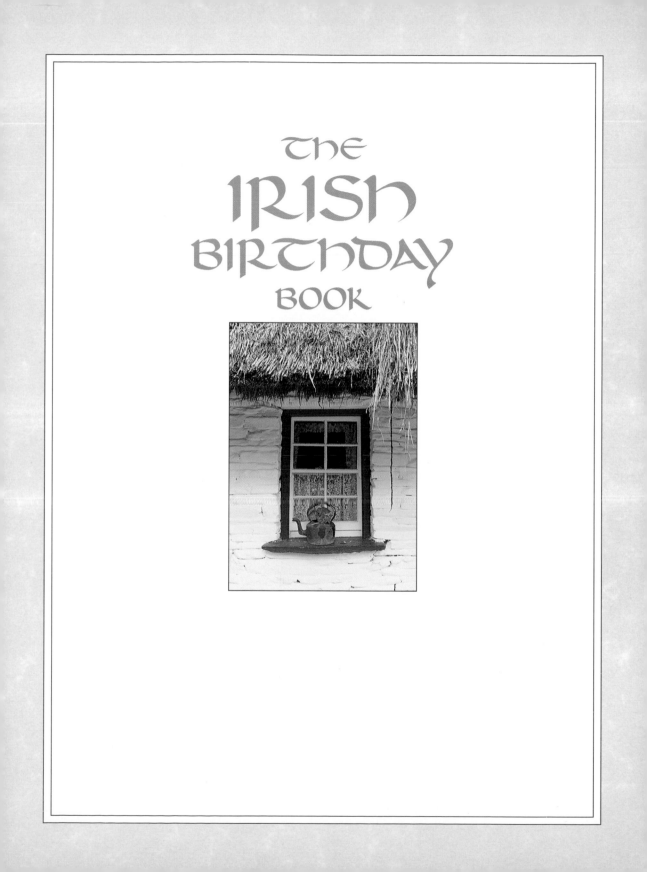

TEXT RESEARCH
Louis Bell

EDITOR
Fleur Robertson

PHOTOGRAPHY
Art Resource, New York
Colour Library Books Ltd
Fine Art Photographic Ltd, London
The National Gallery of Ireland, Dublin
The National Library of Ireland, Dublin
Michael Diggin Photography, Tralee
Pyms Gallery, London
The Slide File, Dublin
Picturepoint Ltd, Windsor

DESIGN
Sally Hiller

TYPESETTING
Sally Hiller
Fleur Robertson

PRODUCTION
Ruth Arthur
Sally Connolly
Neil Randles
Jonathan Tickner

DIRECTOR OF PRODUCTION
Gerald Hughes

Published in Ireland by
Gill & Macmillan Ltd
Goldenbridge, Dublin 8,
with associated companies throughout the world
3424
© 1994 Quadrillion Publishing Ltd
Godalming, Surrey, England
Printed and bound in Italy
ISBN 0 7171 2145 3

THE IRISH BIRTHDAY BOOK

Gill & Macmillan

Still south I went and west and south again
Through Wicklow from the morning till the night,
And far from cities and the sites of men,
Lived with the sunshine and the moon's delight.

Prelude – J.M. Synge

January

Gleann na nGealt, Dingle Peninsula, Co. Kerry

Birthstone:
Garnet

January

1
New Year's Day

1767 Birth of Maria Edgeworth, novelist, best known for *Castle Rackrent*, in Black Bourton, Oxfordshire
1973 Ireland joins the EEC

2

1895 Birth of John Ford, Irish-American film director

3

1925 Birth of Maureen Potter, actress and comedienne
1984 Michael Mills takes office as the first Ombudsman in the Republic of Ireland

4

5

1826 Separate Irish currency abolished, to be replaced by sterling.

6
Epiphany

1839 'Night of the Big Wind': exceptional storms and gales lash Ireland

7

A growing moon and a flowing tide are lucky times to marry in

A Fisherman with Pollan Charles Lamb (1893-1965)

January

8

1876 Birth of Lucien Bull, inventor of electro-cardiograph, in Dublin

9

1929 Birth of Brian Friel, playwright

10

1889 Birth of Maurice Collis, author and painter, in Dublin

11

She who fills the heart, fills the eye

12

1923 Oliver St John Gogarty, writer, surgeon and wit, escapes his Civil War captors by swimming the Liffey and later makes an offering of two swans to the river in thanksgiving

13

1880 Birth of Alexander Brenon, early film director, in Co. Dublin

14

You'll live during the year, for we were just talking of you

The Halfpenny Bridge, Dublin

January

15
1920 First use of proportional representation in Ireland, in local elections

16
1922 Michael Collins takes over control of Dublin Castle from the British authorities on behalf of the new Irish state

17
1860 Birth of Douglas Hyde, scholar, founder of the Gaelic League and first President of the Republic of Ireland, in Castlerea, Co. Roscommon

18
1822 Theatre Royal in Hawkins St, Dublin, opens

19

20
1908 Opening of Municipal Art Gallery, Parnell Square, Dublin

21
1876 Birth of James Larkin, trade unionist, in Liverpool
1919 First meeting of Dail Eireann

A 13th-century bridge over the River Funshion, Co. Cork

January

22

1913 Birth of William Conway, later Cardinal Archbishop of Armagh, in Belfast

23

1834 Opening of St Vincent's Hospital, Dublin

24

1933 General election gives Fianna Fail first-ever overall majority

25

1627 Birth of Robert Boyle, son of the Great Earl of Cork, and inventor of Boyle's Law, at Lismore Castle, Co. Waterford

26

1904 Birth of Sean MacBride, patriot and statesman, in Paris
1907 First night of J.M. Synge's *Playboy of the Western World* at the Abbey Theatre, Dublin

27

1885 Charles Stewart Parnell turns the first sod for the West Clare Railway

28

1952 Birth of Pat Kenny, broadcaster

A storm at Slea Head, Dingle Peninsula, Co. Kerry

January

29

1985 Patrick McEntee SC is admitted to the Northern Ireland inner bar as a QC, the first person from the south to hold such a position since partition

30

1845 Birth of Katharine Wood, better known as Kitty O'Shea, mistress and later wife of Parnell, in Bradwell, Essex

31

1547 Storm damages cathedral at Clonmacnoise
1969 Closure of last colliery in Castlecomer coal field

The kisses of Angus came to me –
And three bright birds on my apple-tree
Pipe their magical haunting song
That shall fill with dreaming my whole life long.

The Kisses of Angus
Ethna Carbery

A lone cottage near Sally Gap in the Wicklow Mountains

I give you the smell of Norman stone, the squelch
Of bog beneath your boots, the red bog-grass,
The vivid chequer of the Antrim hills, the troughs of dark
Golden water for the carthorses, the brass
Belt of serene sun upon the Lough.

Train to Dublin – Louis MacNiece

February

Bogland on the Ring of Kerry road, Co. Kerry

Birthstone:
Amethyst

February

1

First Day of Spring

1859 Birth of Victor Herbert, Irish-American composer
1872 First Dublin trams in service

2

1882 Birth of James Joyce, novelist, in Dublin

3

1729 Laying of foundation stone for new Parliament House (now Bank of Ireland), College Green, Dublin

4

1868 Birth of Countess Constance Markievicz, née Gore-Booth, patriot and first woman Member of the British Parliament

5

1829 Coombe Lying-in Hospital opens

6

1911 Birth of Ronald Reagan, Irish-American and 40th President of the USA

7

1875 Birth of Sir Alfred Chester Beatty, philanthropist and first honorary citizen of Ireland, in New York City

Crofters' Cottages Paul Henry (1876-1958)

February

8
1926 First performance of Sean O'Casey's *The Plough and the Stars* at the Abbey leads to rioting three nights later

9
1854 Birth of Edward Carson, lawyer and political leader, in Dublin
1923 Birth of Brendan Behan, playwright, in Dublin

10
1959 Formation of Irish Congress of Trade Unions

11
1984 Closure of Royal Hibernian Hotel, Dublin

12
1881 First public meeting of the Land League at Claremorris, Co. Mayo
1898 Birth of Frank Aiken, revolutionary and politician, in Camlough, Co. Armagh

13

14
Saint Valentine's Day

1895 First performance of Wilde's *The Importance of Being Earnest*

Clifden, Connemara, Co. Galway

February

15

1874 Birth of Ernest Shackleton, explorer, in Kilkea, Co. Kildare
1971 Decimal Day, as old coinage is changed for decimal currency

16

17

1980 The Derrynaflan Chalice and other ancient treasure discovered in Co. Tipperary

May the strength of three be in your journey

18

19

1904 Birth of Muiris O Suilleabhain author of *Fiche Bliain Ag Fas* (*Twenty Years A-Growing*), on the Great Blasket Island, Co. Kerry

20

1882 Birth of Padraic O Conaire, writer, in Galway

21

1760 French Admiral Thurot sails to Carrickfergus, Co. Antrim, which he occupies for three days
1822 Birth of Richard Southwell Bourke, 6th Earl of Mayo and Viceroy of India, in Dublin

The Mirror Sir William Orpen (1878-1931)

February

22

1832 First burial in Glasnevin Cemetery, Dublin

23

A little bit of anything isn't worth a pin; but a wee bit of sense is worth a lot

24

1841 Birth of John Philip Holland, the inventor of the submarine, in Co. Clare

25

1951 Birth of Neil Jordan, writer and film director

26

1839 Birth of John Pentland Mahaffy, scholar, wit and Provost of Trinity College Dublin, in Switzerland

27

Pity him who makes his opinion a certainty

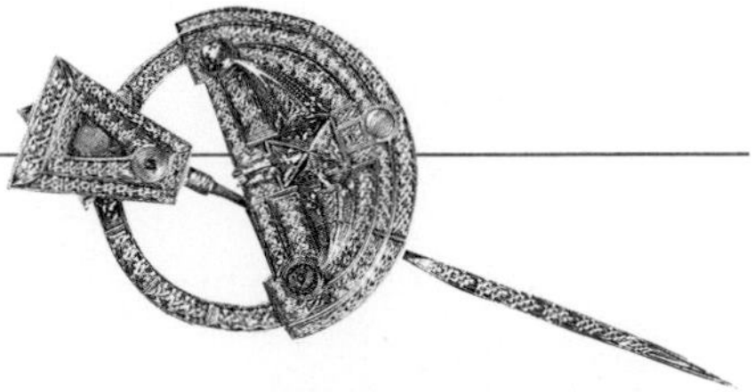

28/29

Traditional turf stack near Mount Errigal, Co. Donegal

In a field by a river my love and I did stand
And on my leaning shoulder she laid her snow-white hand.
She bid me take life easy, as the grass grows on the weirs
But I was young and foolish, and now am full of tears.

Down by the Salley Gardens – W.B. Yeats

March

Castletown House, Co. Kildare

Birthstones:
Aquamarine or Bloodstone

March

1

Saint David's Day

2

3

1786 Foundation stone laid for Four Courts, Dublin

4

1864 Birth of Daniel Mannix, Archbishop of Melbourne, in Charleville, Co. Cork

5

6

1935 Birth of Ronnie Delany, gold medal winner in the 1500 metres at the 1956 Olympic Games in Melbourne

7

1736 Birth of Marie-Louise O'Morphi, courtesan, mistress of King Louis XV of France and model for the painter Boucher

Though wisdom is good in the beginning, it is better at the end

Co. Mayo cottages

March

8

1905 Dungannon Clubs, a nationalist group, founded in Belfast by Bulmer Hobson

9

If you put a silk dress on a goat, he's a goat still

10

1977 The State acquires Barretstown Castle in Co. Kildare

11

1596 Gunpowder explosion kills over 100 people in Winetavern Street, Dublin

12

1685 Birth of George Berkeley, philosopher, at Dysart Castle, Co. Kilkenny

13

1979 Republic of Ireland joins the European Monetary System and breaks the link with sterling

14

1985 Two schoolchildren in Asdee, Co. Kerry, report that local Marian statue had 'moved', the first of a rash of such 'sightings' in Munster that year

Spring Sir John Lavery (1856-1941)

March

15

1790 Foundation of the Sick and Indigent Roomkeepers' Society, Ireland's oldest surviving charity

16

1896 First use of X-Rays in Ireland, at Dr Steevens's Hospital, Dublin

17

Saint Patrick's Day

1779 First St Patrick's Day parade in New York City
1917 Birth of Joseph Locke, singer

18

1800 Birth of Harriet Constance Smithson, afterwards Madame Berlioz, in Ennis, Co. Clare
1949 Birth of Alex Higgins, snooker player

19

Saint Joseph's Day

1824 Birth of William Allingham, poet, in Ballyshannon, Co. Donegal

20

21

1970 Dana (Rosemary Brown) from Derry is Ireland's first winner of the Eurovision Song Contest singing 'All Kinds of Everything'

Scrabo Tower, Co. Down

March

22

1848 Birth of Sarah Purser, artist, at Kingstown, Co. Dublin

23

1948 Rinty Monaghan of Belfast knocks out Jackie Paterson of Glasgow to become the World Flyweight champion

24

Time and patience would bring a snail to Jerusalem

25

Lady Day

1978 John Treacy wins the World Cross-country Championship

26

1986 Australian artist Sidney Nolan announces a bequest of 50 paintings to Ireland

27

1839 Birth of John Ballance, later Prime Minister of New Zealand, in Glenavy, Co. Antrim
1766 Publication of *The Vicar of Wakefield* by Oliver Goldsmith

28

1686 First pensioners admitted to the Royal Hospital, Kilmainham

A shepherd and his dog, Co. Donegal

March

29

1859 First publication of *The Irish Times*

30

31

1871 Birth of Arthur Griffith, patriot and statesman, in Dublin

Long, long ago, beyond the misty space
Of twice a thousand years
In Erin old there dwelt a mighty race
Taller than Roman spears;
Like oaks and towers they had a giant grace
Were fleet as deers
With wind and waves they made their biding place
These western shepherd seers.

The Celts
Thomas D'Arcy McGee

A round tower and crannog, the Irish National Heritage Park, Co. Tyrone

I will arise and go now, for always night and day
I hear lake water lapping with low sounds by the shore;
While I stand on the roadway, or on the pavements grey,
I hear it in the deep heart's core.

The Lake Isle of Innisfree – W.B. Yeats

April

Glengarriff Bay, Co. Cork

Birthstone:

Diamond

April

1

All-fools' Day

1911 Launch of the *Titanic* from Harland & Wolff shipyard, Belfast

2

1902 First production of Yeats' *Cathleen ni Houlihan* starring Maud Gonne
1989 Mikhail Gorbachev visits Ireland

3

1798 Birth of John Banim, novelist, playwright and poet, in Kilkenny
1900 Oldest surviving moving film in Ireland shows Queen Victoria's last visit to Dublin

4

1838 The *Sirius* leaves Cork for New York to become the first ship to make the Atlantic crossing completely under steam
1951 Birth of Twink (Adele King), popular singer and actress

5

1900 Birth of Spencer Tracy, Irish-American film actor
1855 Completion of the Dublin-Belfast railway line

6

7

1868 Thomas D'Arcy McGee, poet and Young Irelander, assassinated in Ottawa

Cork City Hall

April

8

1816 Birth of Sir Frederick William Burton, painter, in Corofin, Co. Clare

A gentle answer quenches anger

9

10

1838 Fr Mathew's temperance campaign begins
1881 Birth of William Leech, painter, in Dublin

11

1864 Opening of Synge St Christian Brothers School, Dublin

12

1928 The aircraft *Bremen*, piloted by Col. James Fitzmaurice and two Germans, takes off from Baldonnel and makes the first east-west transatlantic flight

13

1906 Birth of Samuel Beckett, Nobel Prizewinner for Literature, at Foxrock, Co. Dublin
1742 First performance of Handel's *Messiah* in Fishamble Street, Dublin

14

The Sunshade William Leech (1881-1968)

April

15

1848 First-ever presentation of the green, white and orange tricolour at a meeting of the Irish Confederation
1864 First modern-style Royal Dublin Society Spring Show

16

1871 Birth of John Millington Synge, playwright, at Newtown, Co. Dublin
1752 First regular Dublin-Belfast stagecoach

17

1875 Charles Stewart Parnell first elected to House of Commons as MP for Co. Meath
1936 Birth of Brendan Kennelly, poet

18

1949 Formal declaration of Republic of Ireland

19

20

1896 First screening of a moving film in Ireland at Dan Lowrey's Star of Erin Palace of Varieties (now the Olympia Theatre), Dame Street, Dublin

21

1947 Shannon Airport becomes the world's first duty-free airport

A cottage window, Mallow, Co. Cork

April

22

1894 Birth of Evie Hone, stained glass artist, at Roebuck Grove, Co. Dublin

23

24

1916 Easter Rising

25

Saint Mark's Day

1819 Birth of Vere Foster, nineteenth-century philanthropist and educational reformer

26

1979 Grainne Cronin becomes the first woman to pilot an Aer Lingus scheduled service when she takes charge of the Frankfurt-Shannon flight

27

1904 Birth of Cecil Day-Lewis, poet and critic, in Ballintubber, Co. Mayo

28

A soft-dropping April brings milk to cows and sheep

Mountain sheep

April

29

1888 First All-Ireland football final. Limerick Commercials beat Dundalk Young Irelanders 1-4 to 0-3 in a 21-a-side game

30

When all things spoke the potato said 'Set me warm, dig me warm, eat me warm, that's all I want'

My heart would lighten to see Loch Gréine,
the land, the view, the sky horizon,
the sweet and delightful set of mountains
looming their heads up over each other.
It would brighten a heart worn out with time,
or spent, or faint, or filled with pain
– or the withered, the sour, without wealth or means –
to gaze for a while across the woods
at the shoals of ducks on the cloudless bay
and a swan between them, sailing with them,
at fishes jumping on high for joy,
the flash of a stripe-bellied glittering perch,
the hue of the lake, the blue of the waves
heavy and strong as they rumble in.

<u>The Midnight Court</u>
Brian Merriman

Mount Brandon, Conor Pass, Co. Kerry

'Tis down by the lake where the wild tree fringes its sides,
The maid of my heart, the fair one of Heaven resides –
I think as at eve she wanders its mazes along,
The birds go to sleep by the sweet wild twist of her song.

The Outlaw of Loch Lene – Jeremiah Joseph Callanan

May

Lough Derryclare, Co. Galway

Birthstone:
Emerald

May

1

Saint Philip and Saint James's Day

1769 Birth of Arthur Wellesley, Duke of Wellington, soldier and statesman, in Dublin
1891 Opening of Dublin Loop Line railway bridge

2

1858 Birth of Edith Somerville, novelist, in Corfu
1856 Birth of Matt Talbot, servant of God

3

1785 First meeting of Irish Academy (Royal Irish Academy from 1786)

4

1773 Art O'Leary killed by British soldiers at Carraig an Ime, near Macroom, Co. Cork, which moved his widow Eileen O'Leary to compose her famous lament

5

1914 Birth of Tyrone Power, Irish-American film actor
1888 First publication of *The Irish Catholic* newspaper

6

1820 Birth of Robert Burke, Australian explorer, in St Cleran's, Co. Galway
1934 World premiere of Robert Flaherty's film *Man of Aran*

7

1865 Birth of John MacBride, a leader in the 1916 Rising, in Westport, Co. Mayo
1931 Foundation of An Oige, Irish Youth Hostel Association

Self-portrait Margaret Clarke (1888-1961)

May

8

World Red Cross Day

9

1917 First successful use of the electoral slogan 'Put him in to get him out' wins the Longford South by-election for Joseph McGuinness who was then in Lewes jail in Sussex

10

1960 Birth of Bono (Paul Hewson), lead singer with U2
1972 Republic of Ireland votes 5-1 to join EEC

11

An inch is a great deal on a nose

12

1712 Work begins on the construction of the Old Library in Trinity College Dublin
1950 Birth of Gabriel Byrne, actor

13

1957 First Dublin Theatre Festival opens
1982 Tras Honan elected the first female Cathaoirleach of the Seanad

14

1755 Birth of George Barrington, gentleman pickpocket and author, in Maynooth, Co. Kildare

Scots pines and rhododendrons, Muckross National Park, Co. Kerry

May

15

1808 Birth of Michael William Balfe, composer, best known for *The Bohemian Girl*, in Dublin

16

1920 Start of three-day 'soviet' by workers at Knocklong creamery, Co. Limerick

17

1915 Birth of Oisin Kelly, sculptor, in Dublin
1931 Foundation of Muintir na Tire, a rural development organisation

18

1939 First aircraft lands at the new Rineanna Airfield, Co. Clare, (later Shannon Airport)

19

20

1932 Amelia Earhart lands at Culmore, Co. Derry, to become the first woman to fly the Atlantic solo

21

1944 Birth of Mary Robinson, President of Ireland
1956 Birth of Sean Kelly, world champion cyclist, in Carrick-on-Suir, Co. Tipperary

Cliffs of Moher, Co. Clare

May

22

1946 Birth of George Best footballer, in Belfast

23

1754 Birth of William Drennan, popular poet, the first person to call Ireland the 'Emerald Isle', in Belfast

24

1844 Foundation stone laid for Amiens St railway station, Dublin (now Connolly)

25

1842 Birth of Helen Blackburn, pioneer of feminism, on Valentia Island, Co. Kerry

26

1873 Trinity College Dublin abolishes all remaining religious tests for entry, except for the Divinity Faculty

27

1960 Last barge on Grand Canal leaves James's St harbour with a cargo of Guinness for Limerick

28

Going Downstream David Woodlock (1842-1929)

May

29

1917 Birth of John Fitzgerald Kennedy, Irish-American and the 35th President of the USA

30

1986 Official opening of Connacht Regional Airport at Knock, Co. Mayo, now Horan International Airport

31

1979 Radio Telefis Eireann Radio 2 (now 2 FM) comes on the air for the first time

My love and my delight
The day I saw you first
Beside the market house
I had eyes for nothing else
And love for none but you

The Lament for Art O'Leary
Eileen O'Leary

Cork city from St Patrick's Hill

The cresses on the water and the sorrels are at hand
And the cuckoo's calling daily his note of mimic bland
And the bold thrush sings so bravely his song i' the forests grand
On the fair hills of holy Ireland.

The Fair Hills of Ireland – Samuel Ferguson

June

Glenveagh National Park, Co. Donegal

Birthstones:
Agate, Pearl, Moonstone or Alexandrite

June

1

1852 Submarine telegraph cable from Holyhead to Howth links Britain and Ireland for the first time

2

1973 Irish Continental Line begin their Rosslare-Le Havre car ferry service

3

1981 The Irish-bred racehorse Shergar wins the English Derby by the greatest-ever margin

4

1949 Birth of Alan Stanford, actor

5

1868 Birth of James Connolly, trade unionist and patriot, in Edinburgh
1880 Birth of William Thomas Cosgrave, statesman, in Dublin

6

1913 Birth of Patrick Campbell, author and broadcaster, in Dublin
1800 First priests ordained at Maynooth College

7

1899 Birth of Elizabeth Bowen, novelist, in Dublin
1892 Birth of Kevin O'Higgins, statesman, in Stradbally, Co. Laois

Thoroughbreds at the Irish National Stud, Co. Kildare

June

8

1985 Barry McGuigan beats Eusebio Pedrosa in London to win the World Featherweight Championship

9

1888 Birth of Basil Brooke, later Lord Brookeborough, Prime Minister of Northern Ireland between 1943–63, in Colebrook, Co. Fermanagh

10

11

1990 Republic of Ireland plays first-ever match in the finals of the World Cup, drawing 1-1 with England in Cagliari, Sardinia

12

1987 Opening of National Heritage Park at Ferrycarrig, Co. Wexford

13

1865 Birth of William Butler Yeats, poet and Nobel Prizewinner for Literature, in Dublin

14

1884 Birth of John McCormack, operatic and concert tenor, at Athlone, Co. Westmeath

St Patrick's Cathedral, Dublin

June

15
World Children's Day

1914 First publication of James Joyce's *A Portrait of the Artist as a Young Man*

16

1773 Foundation stone laid for the King's Hospital (the Bluecoat School), Dublin – now the Incorporated Law Society

17

1988 Unveiling of the Smurfit Memorial Fountain in O'Connell St, Dublin, showing the reclining figure of Anna Livia, quickly nicknamed 'the Floozie in the Jacuzzi'

18

1859 Birth of Walter Osborne, painter, at Rathmines, Dublin

19

20

1763 Birth of Theobald Wolfe Tone, patriot, in Dublin
1924 Birth of Audie Murphy, Irish-American actor

21
Midsummer

1854 Irishman David Lucas wins the first-ever Victoria Cross in the Crimean War

Children in Church Walter Osborne (1859-1903)

June

22

1866 Paul Cullen appointed first-ever Irish cardinal by Pope Pius IX

23

1838 Birth of Sir James Gildea, co-founder of the St John's Ambulance Association, at Kilmaine, Co. Mayo
1945 Birth of Paul Costelloe, fashion designer

24

Saint John the Baptist's Day

1834 Over 200 killed and hundreds injured in faction fight at Ballyveigh Strand, Co. Kerry
1895 Birth of Jack Dempsey, Irish-American boxer

25

1783 Bank of Ireland opens to the public for the first time

26

27

1846 Birth of Charles Stewart Parnell, patriot and politician, at Avondale, Co. Wicklow

28

1853 Announcement of proposal to introduce first Irish income tax

Westport House, Co. Mayo

June

29

Saint Peter's Day

1820 The Dublin Society becomes the Royal Dublin Society

30

1986 King Juan Carlos and Queen Sophia of Spain arrive in Ireland for a state visit

Broom out the floor now, lay the fender by,
And plant this bee-sucked bough of woodbine there
And let the window down. The butterfly
Floats in upon the sunbeam, and the fair
Tanned face of June, the nomad gypsy, laughs
Above her widespread wares, the while she tells
The farmer's fortunes in the fields, and quaffs
The water from the spider-peopled wells.

June
Francis Ledwidge

A cottage in Ballymascanlan, Co. Louth, one of Ireland's smallest villages

Sweet was the sound, when oft at evening's close
Up yonder hill the village murmur rose;
There, as I pass'd with careless steps and slow,
The mingling notes came soften'd from below ...

The Village – Oliver Goldsmith

July

Summer Cove, near Kinsale, Co. Cork

Birthstone:
Ruby

July

1
1867 Thomas Francis Meagher, orator, former member of the Young Ireland movement and then temporary governor of Montana, drowns in the River Missouri

2
1900 Birth of Sir Tyrone Guthrie, theatre producer
1964 Opening of the Ulster Folk and Transport Museum at Cultra, Co. Down

3
Saint Thomas' Day

1746 Birth of Henry Grattan, patriot and orator, in Dublin

4
1845 Birth of Thomas John Barnardo, founder of Dr Barnardo's Homes for Children, in Dublin
1928 Birth of Stephen Boyd, actor

5
1790 First Irish mail coach service established
1936 Birth of Tony O'Reilly, rugby player and businessman

6

7
1823 Birth of Francis Fowke, architect of the National Gallery of Ireland, in Ballysillane, Co. Antrim

White Roses Grace Henry (1868-1953)

July

8

9

1959 Mary Browne of Castlerea, Co. Roscommon, becomes the first ban gharda (policewoman)

10

1900 Birth of Paul Vincent Carroll, playwright, in Blackrock, near Dundalk, Co. Louth
1949 Last-ever tram leaves from Nelson Pillar, Dublin

11

1817 Act of Parliament establishes first public lunatic asylums in Ireland

12

1796 First-ever Orange celebrations of the 'Twelfth', the Protestant victory at the Battle of the Boyne, 1690

13

1985 Live Aid concert, organised by Bob Geldof, raises £45 million for Third World famine victims

14

When you go forth to find a wife, leave your eyes at home but take both ears with you

A cottage interior

July

15
Saint Swithin's Day

1907 Birth of Seamus Murphy, sculptor and author of *Stone Mad*, at Greenhill, near Mallow, Co. Cork

16
1985 Viking artefacts from Wood Quay site in Dublin go on exhibition in the National Museum for the first time

17
1871 Birth of John Miller Andrews, second Prime Minister of Northern Ireland

18
1951 Fire destroys the old Abbey Theatre in Dublin

19

Sow early and mow early

20

21
1928 Birth of John B. Keane, playwright, in Listowel, Co. Kerry

The Sonnet William Mulready (1786-1863)

July

22
1817 William Sadler makes first balloon crossing of the Irish Sea

23
1803 Robert Emmet's uprising in Dublin begins and ends in a day

24
1986 Bob Geldof knighted

25
Saint James's Day

1637 Christopher Wandesford begins coal mining at Castlecomer, Co. Kilkenny

26
1856 Birth of George Bernard Shaw, playwright, in Dublin
1987 Stephen Roche becomes the first Irishman to win the Tour de France

27
1866 Completion of the transatlantic telegraph cable from Valentia Island, Co. Kerry, to Newfoundland

28

Pilgrims climb Croagh Patrick, Co. Mayo, on the last Sunday in July

July

29

30

1928 Dr Pat O'Callaghan wins independent Ireland's first-ever Olympic gold medal in the hammer event in Amsterdam

31

1834 First Dublin-Kingstown (Dun Laoghaire) train, horse drawn

At early dawn I once had been
Where Len's blue waters flow,
When summer bid the groves be green
The lamp of light to glow.
As on by bower, and town, and tower,
And widespread fields I stray,
I meet a maid in the greenwood shade
At the dawning of the day.

The Dawning of the Day
Edward Walsh

Yeats' Thoor Ballylee, Co. Galway

There was not in the wide world a valley so sweet
As that vale in whose bosom the bright waters meet;
Oh! the last rays of feeling and life must depart,
Ere the bloom of that valley shall fade from my heart.

The Meeting of the Waters – Thomas Moore

August

A view from Mount Gabriel in west Cork

Birthstones:
Peridot or Sardonyx

August

1

1906 Opening of Belfast City Hall
1931 Birth of Sean O Riada, musician and composer

2

1820 Birth of John Tyndall, scientist and Alpine mountaineer, at Leighlinbridge, Co. Carlow

3

1932 Birth of Peter O'Toole, actor, in Connemara, Co. Galway
1938 Birth of Terry Wogan, star of TV and radio, in Limerick

4

1805 Birth of William Rowan Hamilton, celebrated mathematician, in Dublin

5

1934 Birth of Gay Byrne, broadcaster extraordinaire

6

1775 Birth of Daniel O'Connell, the 'Liberator', near Cahirciveen, Co. Kerry
1830 Opening of first Dublin Horse Show

7

Don't take the thatch off your own house to buy slates for another man's roof

Buttevant Horse Fair, Co. Cork

August

8

1953 Opening of Chester Beatty Library, Dublin
1976 Peace Movement formed in Northern Ireland

9

1979 First Vietnamese 'boat people' arrive to live in Ireland

10

Every mother thinks it is on her own child the sun rises

11

12

1821 King George IV arrives in Ireland for an official visit in an extremely drunken condition

13

1819 Birth of George G. Stokes, one of the finest mathematicians of the century, at Skreen, Co. Sligo

14

1903 Wyndham's Land Act effectively solves the Irish land question by creating private family farms

Dromineer Castle at dawn, Co. Tipperary

August

15
Feast of the Assumption of the Virgin Mary

1808 Foundation of the Christian Brothers

16
1882 Charles Stewart Parnell made a Freeman of the city of Dublin

17
1920 Birth of Maureen O'Hara, actress

18
1861 First Sunday opening of the Botanic Gardens, Dublin, to the public

19
1887 Birth of Francis Ledwidge, poet, at Slane, Co. Meath

20
1778 Birth of Bernardo O'Higgins, 'father' of Chilean independence
1818 Birth of John Ball, scientist and Alpine traveller, in Dublin

21
1854 Last-ever Donnybrook Fair

The Italian Gardens, Garinish Island, Co. Cork

August

22

'Time enough' never cut the barley

23

1912 Birth of Gene Kelly, Irish-American dancer and actor
1972 Lord Killanin becomes the first Irish President of the International Olympic Committee

24

Saint Bartholomew's Day

1747 Birth of William La Touche, philanthropist and founder of the first Dublin bank, in Dublin

25

1882 Birth of Sean T. O'Kelly, second president of the Republic of Ireland, in Dublin

26

1913 First day of the Great Lock-Out in Dublin

27

1798 French General Humbert wins the 'Races of Castlebar' when his troops rout the local British garrison

28

1872 First horse-drawn tramcars in service in Belfast

Sewing in the Shade Sir John Lavery (1856-1941)

August

29

1871 Birth of Jack B. Yeats,
painter, in London
1890 Opening of National
Library of Ireland

30

1841 First published edition of
The Cork Examiner

31

1945 Birth of Van Morrison, rock
superstar, in Belfast

Late August, given heavy rain and sun
For a full week, the blackberries would ripen.
At first, just one, a glossy purple clot
Among others, red, green, hard as a knot.
You ate that first one and its flesh was sweet
Like thickened wine: summer's blood was in it
Leaving stains upon the tongue and lust for picking.

Blackberry Picking
Seamus Heaney

Late summer on the Iveragh Peninsula, Co. Kerry

Limestone and basalt and a whitewashed house
With passages of great stone flags
And a walled garden with plums on the wall
And a bird piping in the night ...

Cushendun – Louis MacNiece

September

Sneem, a noted angling centre on the Kenmare River, Co. Kerry

Birthstone:
Sapphire

September

1

1830 Dublin Zoo opens
1856 Birth of John Redmond, political leader, at Ballytrent, Co. Wexford
1864 Birth of Sir Roger Casement, patriot, at Sandycove, Co. Dublin

2

3

1850 Establishment of Queen's Colleges in Belfast, Cork and Galway (now Queen's University, University College Cork and University College Galway)

4

1989 Century Radio, Ireland's first national commercial station, goes on the air

5

1911 Formation of the Irish Women Workers' Union

6

1813 Birth of Isaac Butt, patriot, at Glenfin, Co. Donegal
1965 Birth of Christopher Nolan, author, at Mullingar, Co. Westmeath

7

1984 Restoration of the Royal Hospital, Kilmainham completed by the Office of Public Works

University College Galway

September

8
1908 St Enda's School opens under the headmastership of Patrick Pearse

Time used sharpening a scythe is not time wasted

9

10
1763 First publication of *The Freeman's Journal*
1981 Opening of National Concert Hall, Dublin

11
1855 Ireland play their first-ever cricket international, in which they beat England

12
1907 Birth of Louis MacNiece, poet, in Belfast

13
1907 Opening of Tara St Fire Station, Dublin

14
1889 A Mr Spencer becomes the first Irish person to make a parachute jump when he leaps out of a balloon and lands safely at Clonturk Park, Dublin

Hide and Go Seek Samuel McCloy (1831-1904)

September

15

16

1925 Birth of Charles J. Haughey, Taoiseach

17

1711 Birth of John Zephaniah Holwell, in Dublin, later one of the survivors of the Black Hole of Calcutta
1934 Birth of Maureen Connolly, Irish-American tennis star

18

May the Lord keep you in his hand and never close his fist too tight on you

19

1803 The patriot Robert Emmet's speech from the dock prior to execution: 'When my country takes her place among the nations of the earth, then, and not till then, let my epitaph be written'

20

1588 Three ships of the Spanish Armada run aground at Streedagh, Co. Sligo

21

1881 Birth of Eamonn Ceannt, signatory of 1916 Proclamation, at Glenamaddy, Co. Galway

Saint Matthew's Day

Digging for lugworms

September

22

1788 Thomas 'Buck' Whaley sets out to walk from Dublin to Jerusalem to win a bet, which he succeeds in doing

23

Your son is your son today, but your daughter is your daughter forever

24

1861 Opening of Mater Hospital, Dublin
1896 Birth of F. Scott Fitzgerald, Irish-American writer

25

26

1902 Birth of James Dillon, politician and orator, in Ballaghadereen, Co. Roscommon

27

1972 Opening of the National Institute of Higher Education, Limerick, now the University of Limerick

28

No man ever wore a cravat as nice as his own child's arm around his neck

The Hayfield Rose Barton (1856-1929)

September

29

Michaelmas

1889 Birth of Sean Keating, painter, in Limerick
1979 Pope John Paul II begins the first-ever papal visit to Ireland

30

1959 World premiere of *Mise Eire* at Cork Film Festival, music by Sean O Riada

May she become a flourishing hidden tree
That all her thoughts may like the linnet be,
And have no business but dispensing round
Their magnanimities of sound,
Nor but in merriment begin a chase
Nor but in merriment a quarrel.
O may she live like some green laurel
Rooted in one dear perpetual place.

A Prayer for My Daughter
W.B. Yeats

Gortin Glen Forest Park, Co. Tyrone

The red rose whispers of passion,
And the white rose breathes of love;
O, the red rose is a falcon,
And the white rose is a dove.

A White Rose – John Boyle O'Reilly

October

Bantry Bay from the garden of Bantry House

Birthstones:
Opal or Pink Tourmaline

October

1
1911 Unveiling of Parnell Monument, Dublin
1933 Birth of Richard Harris, film actor

2
1867 Abercorn Basin and Hamilton Dock opened in port of Belfast

3
1980 Miss Justice Mella Carroll becomes first female judge of the Irish High Court

4
1886 Birth of Lennox Robinson, playwright, in Douglas, Co. Cork

5
1911 Birth of Brian O'Nolan, alias Flann O'Brien alias Myles na Gopaleen, writer
1951 Birth of Bob Geldof, rock musician and instigator of Band Aid for famine relief in Africa

6

7

The shakiest tree in the orchard is sometimes the last to fall

A detail of the carving on the High Cross at Moone, Co. Kildare

October

8

1974 Sean MacBride wins the Nobel Prize for Peace

9

Better is a small fish than an empty dish

10

1977 Mairead Corrigan and Betty Williams, founders of the Peace Movement in Northern Ireland, win the Nobel Prize for Peace

11

1866 Opening of Alexandra College for girls, Dublin

12

1876 Birth of Jerome Connor, sculptor, in Anascaul, Co. Kerry

13

1940 Birth of Mick Doyle, rugby international, coach and author

14

1814 Birth of Thomas Davis, poet and patriot, in Mallow, Co. Cork
1882 Birth of Eamon de Valera, statesman, in New York City

Cupboard Love Walter Osborne (1859-1903)

October

15
1842 First publication of *The Nation* newspaper

16
1854 Birth of Oscar Wilde, playwright and wit, in Dublin
1890 Birth of Michael Collins, patriot, in Woodfield, Clonakilty Co. Cork

17
1907 Marconi wireless service begins between Clifden, Co. Galway and Cape Breton, Canada

18
Saint Luke's Day

19
1610 Birth of James Butler, first Duke of Ormond, statesman and soldier
1680 Birth of John Abernethy, founder of Irish Unitarianism

20
May I see you grey and combing your children's hair

21
1879 Foundation of the Land League
1904 Birth of Patrick Kavanagh, poet, in Iniskeen, Co. Monaghan

Time to spare

October

22

1884 First women graduates conferred by the Royal University of Ireland

23

1969 Samuel Beckett wins the Nobel Prize for Literature

24

United Nations' Day

1789 Work starts on the construction of the Royal Canal

25

1899 Birth of Michael MacLiammoir, actor and writer, in Cork

26

1831 Birth of Nathaniel Hone, painter, in Dublin

27

Autumn days come quickly, like the running of a hound upon the moor

28

1986 Computerisation of the Dublin Stock Exchange in the so-called 'Big Bang'

A study in brown: Connemara, Co. Galway

October

29

1945 Last scheduled Pan-Am flying boat leaves Foynes, Co. Limerick for USA

30

1751 Birth of Richard Brinsley Sheridan, playwright and politician, in Dublin

31

1883 Birth of Sara Allgood, actress, in Dublin

Halloween

O Son of God, it would be sweet, a lovely journey,
to cross the wave, the fount in flood, and visit Ireland:
to Eolarg Plain, by Foibne Hill, across Loch Febail,
and listen there to the matching music of the swans.

Flocks of gulls would fill with pleasure as we sailed swiftly
into the welcome of Port na Ferg in our 'Red with Dew'.
I am full of sorrow that I left Ireland when I had my strength
and then grew tearful and full of sadness in a foreign land.

Attributed to St Colum Cille

The Franciscan Friary at Askeaton, Co. Limerick

The long day was bright,
It slowly passed from the purple slopes of the hill;
And then the night
Came floating quietly down, and the world grew still.

Nocturne – Francis Wynne

November

Evening light over Macgillycuddy's Reeks, Killarney, Co. Kerry

Birthstones:
Topaz or Citrine

November

1
All Saints' Day

1978 RTE 2 television (now Network 2) launched

2

1854 Catholic University, the precursor of University College Dublin, opens

3

1951 Opening of first Wexford Opera Festival

4

1972 Dermot Ryan becomes the first Catholic archbishop of Dublin to attend a service in Christ Church Cathedral since the Reformation

5

1855 Charles Gavan Duffy, Young Irelander and co-founder of *The Nation*, emigrates to Australia where he later becomes Prime Minister of Victoria

6

1791 Opening of Dublin's Custom House

7

A Connemara Girl Augustus Burke (c.1838-91)

November

8
1847 Birth of Abraham 'Bram' Stoker, author of *Dracula,* in Dublin

9
1976 Patrick Hillery becomes the 6th President of the Republic of Ireland

10

11
Saint Martin's Day

1925 George Bernard Shaw wins the Nobel Prize for Literature

12
1929 Birth of Grace Kelly, Irish-American actress and later Princess of Monaco
1967 First ROSC exhibition of modern art opens at the Royal Dublin Society

13
1831 Sisters of Mercy established by Catherine McAuley
1863 St Stephen's Green, Dublin, first open to the public

14
1923 W.B. Yeats wins the Nobel Prize for Literature

A cottage interior

November

15
1881 Birth of William Pearse, brother of Patrick and one of the 16 executed in 1916 following the Easter Rising
1946 Formation of the Irish Naval Service

16
1793 Birth of Francis Danby, landscape painter and inventor of new type of ship's anchor, in Killinick, Co. Wexford

17
1930 First Irish Hospital Sweepstakes draw sees first prize of $208,792 shared between three winners

18
1741 George Frederick Handel, composer, arrives in Ireland

19
1954 First performance of *The Quare Fella* by Brendan Behan

20
1719 Birth of Spranger Barry, actor and a rival of David Garrick, in Dublin
1925 Birth of Robert Kennedy, Irish-American US Attorney General

21
1952 Birth of Eamonn Coughlan, athlete

A stream in Tollymore Forest Park, Co. Down

November

22

1912 Birth of Donagh McDonagh, poet, lawyer and author of *Happy as Larry*, in Cloughjordan, Co. Tipperary

23

1841 Birth of Richard 'Boss' Croker, Tammany Hall leader, in Clonakilty, Co. Cork

24

1713 Birth of Laurence Sterne, comic author of *Tristram Shandy*, in Clonmel, Co. Tipperary

25

1764 Birth of Henry Charles Sirr, town-major of Dublin who arrested Robert Emmet

26

1791 First Irish transported convicts arrive in New South Wales, Australia
1910 Birth of Cyril Cusack, actor
1924 Birth of Pat Phoenix, actress

27

1871 Opening of the Gaiety Theatre, Dublin
1878 Birth of Sir William Orpen, painter, in Stillorgan, Co. Dublin

28

1959 Birth of Stephen Roche, the only Irishman to win the Tour de France

The Man from Aranmore Jack B. Yeats (1871-1957)

November

29

1898 Birth of C.S. Lewis, novelist, in Belfast

30

1667 Birth of Jonathan Swift, writer, satirist and Dean of St Patrick's Cathedral, in Dublin

Saint Andrew's Day

Twas the dream of a God
And the mould of his hand,
That you shook 'neath his stroke,
That you trembled and broke
To this beautiful land.

Ireland
Dore Sigerson Shorter

The beach at Moneygold, north of Grange, Co. Sligo

With deep affection and recollection
I often think of the Shandon bells
Whose sounds so wild would, in days of childhood
Fling round my cradle their magic spells.

The Bells of Shandon – F.S. Mahony (Fr Prout)

December

The River Lee, Cork city

Birthstones:
Turquoise or Zircon

December

1

1946 Birth of Gilbert O'Sullivan, musician
1956 Ronnie Delany wins the 1500 metres at the Melbourne Olympic Games

2

1802 Birth of Dominic Corrigan, physician and discoverer of the heart complaint known as 'Corrigan's Pulse'

3

1745 Birth of John Toler, Lord Norbury, notorious legal ignoramus and hanging judge, in Beechwood, Co. Tipperary
1897 Birth of Kate O'Brien, playwright and author

4

1879 Birth of Hamilton Harty, composer and musician, in Hillsborough, Co. Down

5

1905 Opening of electric tram service in Belfast

6

1921 Anglo-Irish Treaty signed in London
1922 Irish Free State established

7

1867 First publication of poem 'God Save Ireland' by T.D. Sullivan in *The Nation*
1888 Birth of Joyce Cary, author, in Derry

Lily (Susan) Yeats John B. Yeats (1839-1922)

December

8

The Immaculate Conception

1939 Birth of James Galway, international flautist, in Belfast

9

1840 Birth of Richard Bagwell, historian, at Clonmel, Co. Tipperary

10

1951 Dr E.T.S. Walton of Trinity College Dublin wins the Nobel Prize for Physics
1960 Birth of Kenneth Branagh, actor and director, in Belfast

11

1905 Birth of Erskine Hamilton Childers, 4th President of the Republic of Ireland, in London

12

Short and sweet, like an ass's trot

13

1960 Inaugural flight of the 'St Patrick', a Boeing 707, Aer Lingus's first jet

14

1874 Formation of the Irish Football Union, precursor of the Irish Rugby Football Union

Lough Derryclare, Co. Galway

December

15
1896 Birth of Monk Gibbon, author, in Dublin
1932 Birth of Edna O'Brien, novelist, in Tuamgraney, Co. Clare

16
1838 Birth of John Gubbins, racehorse owner and breeder whose colt Galty More won the Triple Crown of the 2,000 Guineas, the Derby and the St Leger in 1897

17
1834 First steam train between Dublin and Kingstown (Dun Laoghaire)

18
1891 First publication of *The Irish Daily Independent*, later to become *The Irish Independent*

19

20
1909 Ireland's first cinema, the Volta, opens in Mary St, Dublin, under the managership of James Joyce, the writer
1915 Birth of Noel Browne, politician, doctor and radical

21
1985 Foundation of the Progressive Democrat Party

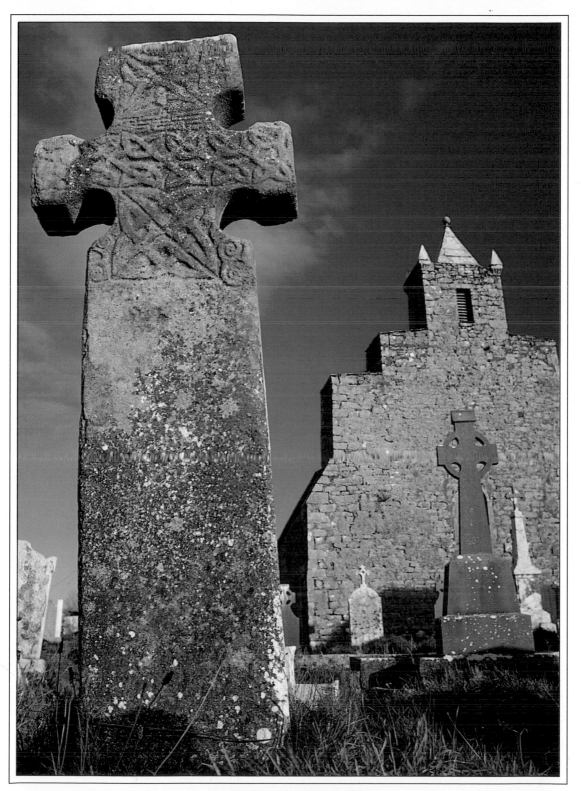

The High Cross at Kilfenora, Co. Clare

December

22

1541 Robert Painswick appointed first Church of Ireland Dean of Christ Church Cathedral, Dublin

23

1834 Last reported sighting of Great Auk in Ireland, off Waterford Harbour
1900 Birth of Noel Purcell, stage and film actor, in Dublin

24
Christmas Eve

25
Christmas Day

1881 Birth of Field-Marshal Sir John Dill, chief of staff of British army in the early days of the Second World War, in Lurgan, Co. Armagh

26
Saint Stephen's Day

1820 Birth of Dion Boucicault, playwright, in Dublin
1870 Statue of William Smith O'Brien, Young Irelander, unveiled in O'Connell St, Dublin

27

1849 Catholic Young Men's Society founded in Limerick
1904 Abbey Theatre, Dublin, opens

28

1970 Pat Taaffe, Ireland's most famous steeplechase jockey – forever associated with the immortal Arkle – retires

A portrait of Christ from the Book of Kells, Trinity College, Dublin

December

29

1908 Foundation of the Irish Transport and General Workers Union, now part of Services Industrial, Professional and Technical Union

30

A misty winter brings a pleasant spring, a pleasant winter a misty spring

31

1961 RTE television begins broadcasting

New Year's Eve

Gentle in the night flows my river, the Liffey.
It is mine by right of love, this river always
Running, since my childhood, under my feet, always
Branching along my veins – this river of birds,
Avenue of serene, Ascendancy swans,
Trail of a single gunman cormorant,
Stage of the seagull's ballet – those faery visitors
Who cry and perch and fly, blown in the air
Like paper toys.

In the City
Rhoda Sinclair Coghill

Seagulls and the Four Courts, Dublin

Anniversaries

1st – Paper or Cotton
2nd – Cotton or Paper
3rd – Leather
4th – Silk or Flowers
5th – Wood
6th – Iron or Candy
7th – Copper or Wool
8th – Bronze or Rubber
9th – Pottery
10th – Tin
11th – Steel
12th – Linen
13th – Lace
14th – Ivory
15th – Crystal
20th – China
25th – Silver
30th – Pearl
40th – Ruby
45th – Sapphire
50th – Gold
55th – Emerald
60th – Diamond
65th – Platinum

Symbolism of Gemstones

Amethyst: humility, sincerity and prevention of drunkenness

Aquamarine: courage and energy

Bloodstone: courage and wisdom

Carbuncle: lucky in love

Crystal: purity and simplicity

Diamond: innocence, success, conjugal affection, unshakeable faith

Emerald: safety in child-bearing, lucky in love, tranquility

Garnet: constancy and truth

Moonstone: drives away nightmares

Onyx: sincerity

Opal: unlucky unless it is the fiancée's birthstone, reflects every mood

Pearl: beautiful bride, but signifies tears

Peridot: kind to husband

Ruby: freedom from care, chastity, glory

Sapphire: chastity and hope

Sardonyx: secures marital happiness

Topaz: cure for sleeplessness, fidelity

Turquoise: love and riches, prevents arguments in matrimony

A Cottage Garden Walter Osborne (1859-1903)

Notes

Notes

Notes

Notes

Lough Corrib Paul Henry (1877-1958)

Photograph and Painting Acknowledgements

ART RESOURCE, NEW YORK Feb 15 (courtesy of The Tate Gallery, London); Mar 8 (courtesy of The Bridgeman Art Library, London and Giraudon, Paris); Jul 15 (courtesy of the V&A Museum, London).
FINE ART PHOTOGRAPHS LTD, LONDON May 22 (courtesy of Marian and John Alway, Datchet); Sept 22 (courtesy of Bill Minns, Farnham).
MICHAEL DIGGIN PHOTOGRAPHY, TRALEE Half title page; Jan opener; Jan 22; Feb opener; Apr 22, both images; May 8; Jun opener; Jun 22 (small picture); Aug opener; Aug 8; Aug 15; Aug 29; Sept opener; Sept 15; Oct 29; Nov opener; Nov 8.

NATIONAL GALLERY OF IRELAND, DUBLIN Apr 8; Nov 1; Nov 22; Dec 1; Anniversaries and Gemstones.
NATIONAL LIBRARY OF IRELAND, DUBLIN Feb 22 cut out.
COURTESY OF PYMS GALLERY, LONDON Jan 1; Feb 1; May 1; Jun 15; Jul 1; Aug 22; Sept 8; Oct 8; above.
THE SLIDE FILE, DUBLIN Jan 15; Jan 29; Feb 8; Feb 22; Mar opener; Mar 1; Mar 29; Apr opener; Apr 1; Apr 15; Apr 29; May opener; May 29; Jun 1; Jun 22 (main picture); Jun 29; Jul opener; Jul 8; Jul 22; Jul 29; Aug 1; Sept 1; Oct opener; Oct 1; Oct 15; Oct 22; Dec opener; Dec 8; Dec 15; facing page.
PICTUREPOINT LTD, WINDSOR Dec 22.

The Mussenden Temple, near Downhill, Co. Antrim